J
305.9
Sen

Senker, Cath.

Why are people
refugees?

DATE		
FEB 2 0 2007		
AUG 0 6 2007		

Why Are People Refugees?

Cath Senker

Raintree

Chicago, Illinois

**Library of Congress Cataloging-in-Publication
Data**
Senker, Cath.
   Why are people refugees? / Cath Senker.
      p. cm. -- (Exploring tough issues)
Summary: Explains what a refugee is, and how
war, persecution, economic
hardship, and natural disasters cause people to
leave their homelands.
Includes bibliographical references and index.
   ISBN 0-7398-6685-0 (Library Binding-hardcover)
   1. Refugees--Juvenile literature. 2. Refugees--
History--Juvenile
literature. [1. Refugees.] I. Title. II. Series.
   JV6346.S46 2004
   305.9'06914--dc22

2003012745

08 07 06 05 04
10 9 8 7 6 5 4 3 2 1
Printed by C&C Offset, China.

Acknowledgments
The author would like to thank the following
for their help in the preparation of this book: Ali
Brownlie, Michael Cardona, Sarah Harland, and
Simba of the Zimbabwe Association for the case
study in chapter 4; Bertha Leverton for the case
study in chapter 2, from *I Came Alone* compiled
by Bertha Leverton and Shmuel Lowensohn (Book
Guild, 1990); Minority Rights Group for the case
studies in chapters 1 and 3; UNHCR magazine
Refugees for the case study in chapter 7.

Picture acknowledgments
The publisher would like to thank the following
for their kind permission to use their pictures:
pp. 2 (top), 5 Rex (Kevin Weaver) p.2 (bottom),
20, 22 Exile Images (M. Kobayashi); p. 4 Exile
Images (J. Hawkins); p. 6 Rex (Kevin McKiernan,
Sipa); p. 8, 23 Rex (Sipa); pp. 12, 13 Hodder
Wayland Picture Library (Imperial War Museum);
p. 9, 30 Popperfoto (Claro Cortes, Reuters); pp. 10,
11, 16 Popperfoto (Corinne Dufka, Reuters); p. 14
Topham Picturepoint; pp. 15, 18, 25, 27, 40, 42, 44
Exile Images (Howard Davies); p. 17, 43 Exile
Images (R. Chalasani); p. 19 Rex (Mark Peters);
p. 21 Exile Images (H. Ruiz); p. 24 Popperfoto
(Gregg Newton, Reuters); p. 26 Popperfoto
(Howard Burditt, Reuters); p. 28 Popperfoto
(Louis Gouliamaki), p. 29 Popperfoto (Jerry
Lampen, Reuters); pp. 31, 32 Camera Press;
p. 33 Popperfoto (Guillermo Granja, Reuters);
p. 34 Rex (Wilhelmsen); p. 35 Popperfoto (Tim
Wimborne, Reuters); p. 36 Hodder Wayland
Picture Library (UNRWA); p. 39 Rex (AA/Sipa);
p. 38 Popperfoto (AFP); p. 41 Popperfoto
(Matthew Green, Reuters); p. 45 The Refugee
Council (Tash Law).

Cover picture: Kurdish refugees in Turkey,
April 10, 1991.
Corbis (Peter Turnley)

Contents

1.Who Is a Refugee?

Forced to flee

Esperanza, age 15, had to escape to another part of Colombia when soldiers killed her father in 1997. Elvira, a 13-year-old, was forced out of her home in Kosovo in 1999 and brought to safety in Britain. Felipe, a 22-year-old Mexican, had been homeless and unemployed since leaving school. He entered the United States illegally in 2001 and found work as a janitor in an office building.

▲ *These children have been forced to leave their homes and move to another part of Colombia in South America because of civil war. They are being cared for by a charity.*

Which of the above are refugees? According to the 1951 United Nations (UN) Refugee Convention, a refugee is someone who has fled from his or her country and cannot return because of his or her "well-founded fear of being persecuted for reasons of race, religion, nationality, membership of a particular social group, or political opinion." Refugees who have been persecuted and claim the right to asylum, a safe haven in the country they've arrived in, are known as asylum seekers.

▲ *These Kosovars had to flee their homes in 1999 after Serb forces took over their land. Most went to nearby countries and some were accepted by Western European nations.*

Esperanza did not leave her country. This makes her an "internally displaced person (IDP)." Felipe was not persecuted but he lived in poverty, so he moved to another country to work. He is known as an "economic migrant." According to the UN definition, the only genuine refugee is Elvira.

This book will look at the many reasons why people are forced to leave their homes, whether because of conflict, fear of persecution, or desperate poverty.

FACT:
Some 21 million people were internally displaced by the end of the 1990s, compared to 13—14 million in 1990. About 12 million people in the world are legally accepted as refugees. Between 75 percent and 80 percent of the approximately 50 million refugees and displaced persons around the world are women and children.

UN High Commissioner for Refugees

Refugees, IDPs, and economic migrants

◀ Mexican farmworkers in the United States. Migrants typically work as agricultural laborers, building workers, or cleaners. They tend to do the jobs that local people prefer not to do.

So what exactly are the differences between these three groups? Refugees and IDPs have been forced to leave home for the same reasons. Usually they live in an area of conflict and are in danger. The difference between IDPs and refugees is that refugees have left their own countries and crossed an international border to another country. IDPs move to another part of their own country. The great majority of refugees move to other poor countries. Most people in both groups come from the poorest countries of the world.

FACT:
One person out of every 115 people alive today is a refugee or displaced person. There are refugees living in every country in the world, but most of them have been taken in by the poorer countries of Africa and Asia. Most of the world's internally displaced people also live in these countries.
Refugee Council, 2002

The issue of economic migrants is a complicated one. People have always moved from country to country to seek work and better opportunities. You might know people whose parents have moved from Europe, Australia, Africa, or Mexico to work in the United States.

Many of the poor people who migrate to richer countries to work do not move only for a better standard of living. For example, Kurds from Turkey have moved in large numbers to Germany to work. Jobs are much better paid there. But life is also difficult and dangerous for Kurds in Turkey, where they are not allowed to speak their own language or practice their culture. Many do not come as refugees, but the difference between economic migrants and refugees is not always clear.

▼ *A map showing the numbers of refugees living in each major region of the world on December 31, 1999. The greatest numbers are in the poorest regions of the world.*

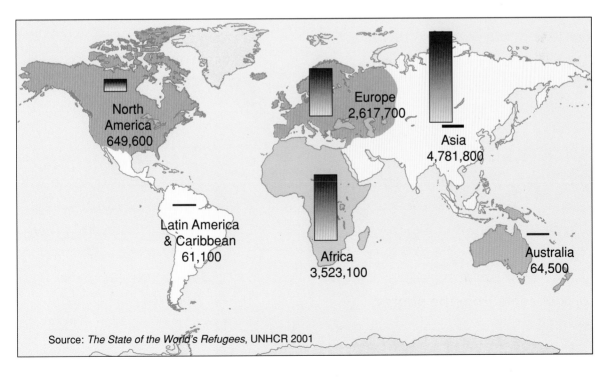

North America 649,600

Europe 2,617,700

Asia 4,781,800

Latin America & Caribbean 61,100

Africa 3,523,100

Australia 64,500

Source: *The State of the World's Refugees*, UNHCR 2001

Child refugees

Imagine having to pack up a few precious things and say goodbye to your home and family, perhaps forever. Over half of the world's refugees are children. Half of them live in Africa, of whom two million live in Sudan. Children might have to flee on their own because their parents have been killed or they have been separated from them. Sometimes the parents send their children away because it is their only chance of survival.

Unaccompanied child refugees and IDPs suffer from particular difficulties. Without anyone to look after them, they are at greater risk from disease and hunger. Adults or older children may abuse them. Some armies recruit refugee children because they are cheap to feed and easy to influence. Sometimes they are forced to become child soldiers, because it is the only way for them to get food.

◄ *Refugee children in Somalia. In refugee camps people may be short of food and have to live in dirty conditions, which puts children at particular risk. Older children often have to take responsibility for caring for younger brothers and sisters.*

Refugee children can suffer from terrible trauma. They may have seen horrendous violent acts. Perhaps they have seen family members brutally murdered. Even if they are lucky enough to reach a refugee camp, there may be no teachers there to educate them. Many children spend years away from their homes, often in different places. The average amount of time a child is displaced is six years in Africa and Asia and seven years in Latin America.

▲ *Afghani refugee girls at a class near Islamabad in Pakistan in 2002. The Afghan government had not allowed girls to go to school.*

case study·case study·case study·case study·case study

"My name's Lul Ugas. When I was a little girl I lived in a town called Howadaag in Somalia. It was great over there. I lived with my mom, dad, brother, and sister. After my father died, I lived with my mom for about a month. Then we children had to travel to Ethiopia because there was fighting in my country.

"We couldn't stay in Ethiopia because it was too expensive, so we moved to Yemen. After two years there was fighting there, so we moved back to Ethiopia for six months. Then we all had to travel to England.

"I would like to live with my mom. I always think of her and I will always remember her."

2.The History of Refugees

Creating borders

People have always moved to seek work or avoid conflict. For most of human history, people only had to cross natural borders, such as oceans, mountains, or deserts. If they came across other people, sometimes they were welcomed. At other times, however, they fought others for the right to use the land. In some countries, rulers built walls to keep out other people. For example, the Great Wall of China was built in the third century BCE to keep out the Mongol people.

The fixing of borders began around 500 years ago when nation-states began to form in Europe. European countries were growing more powerful and developed strong governments to run them. A sense of national identity grew, a belief that people who came from a country belonged there while others did not. For example, in 1601, Queen Elizabeth I forced Africans leave England. It was a time of famine and unemployment, and England's rulers chose to blame Africans for the problems. They were seen as different from the white majority, and therefore they were very easy to target for expulsion.

In the 1600s European powers took control of other parts of the world in a process called colonialism. They seized large parts of Asia, Africa,

"The Queen's majesty ... is highly discontented to understand the great number of Negroes and blackamoors [black Africans] which ... are crept into this realm."

Royal Proclamation, Queen Elizabeth I of England, 1601

10

and the Americas, and they established borders between the lands.

Often, people from different ethnic groups lived in the same land. The rulers tended to favor one group at the expense of another, causing divisions in society. For example, in 19th-century India, the British rulers favored the Hindus over the Muslims. This kind of policy led to conflicts. The conflicts later caused waves of refugees.

▲ *In this early 20th-century photo, servants are waiting on their colonial masters in Bangalore, India. British rulers made local Indians work for them.*

◀ *Muslim refugees pouring out of India and into the new state of Pakistan after the partition of India in 1947. As soon as India was divided, Hindus and Sikhs started killing Muslims in India, and Muslims killed Hindus and Sikhs in Pakistan. It is estimated that about 12 million people switched countries to avoid the violence.*

World War II and its aftermath

World War II caused the biggest movement of refugees the world had seen. When Adolf Hitler rose to power in Germany in 1933, his Nazi government took away Jewish people's rights and forced them out of most jobs. They were arrested and attacked, and their property was burned to the ground. By 1939, half of Germany's Jewish population of 525,000 had emigrated.

Between 1939 and 1941, Hitler invaded many European countries. The Jews were trapped in Nazi-occupied lands and few managed to escape. Other countries did little to help, although people in Denmark, Norway, and France helped Jews to flee. Six million Jews were murdered by the Nazis.

About 60 million people were forced to leave their homes amid the death and destruction caused by World War II. Afterward, the United Nations set up a special organization called the United Nations Relief and Rehabilitation Administration (UNRRA) to help refugees and displaced people to return home.

In the early part of World War II, millions of Jews in Nazi-occupied European countries were forced to move to ghettos in Poland. They were then sent to death camps to be killed. In 1943, people in the Warsaw ghetto rose up against the Nazis but they were defeated.

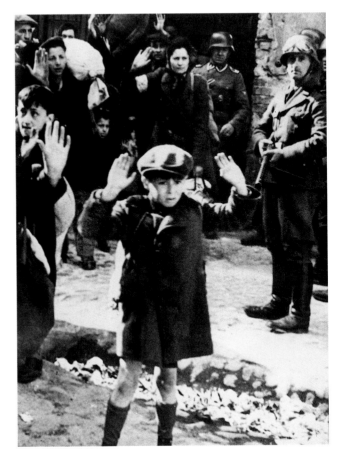

Many people did not want to return, such as the two million Soviet citizens who were unhappy about returning to communist rule. But they were forced to go. Many Jewish people did not want go back to countries where they had been persecuted. Some were allowed to travel to the United States and others managed to get to Palestine in the Middle East.

Modern warfare since 1945 has uprooted people in similar ways and caused huge movements of refugees.

▲ *These refugees returned to Greece after having fled their country during World War II.*

case study·case study·case study·case study·case study

In November 1938, the British government agreed to take 10,000 Jewish children from Nazi Germany. In 1939, one of them, Inge Hack from Nuremberg, Germany, then age thirteen, remembered the experience:

"It was a very sad Hanukkah [the Jewish festival of lights]. My father had been taken away, Mom was sad, and I was waiting for my transport to England. One day we received notice that I was to go at 1 A.M.… We said goodbye, not knowing then that it was the last time we would ever see each other.

"When we went ashore in England, a bus was waiting for us.… Soon we arrived at our camp, which was called Dovercourt.… We spent a lovely time there … One Sunday I received a message to go to London where I was to meet my new foster family.…I packed my bag [and] said goodbye to those left behind, to make the journey to London."

Refugees in recent times

Following World War II, the international community set up a system for helping refugees. The UN Refugee Convention of 1951 provided a definition of refugees (see page 4) and listed their rights, including their right to stay in a safe country and to live, work, and study freely. Since then there have been various refugee crises.

After the war, the Soviet Union took over many countries in Eastern Europe and communist governments were established there. Many people did not want to live under communism. In one of these countries, Hungary, there was an uprising in 1956. It was crushed and some 200,000 refugees fled for safety.

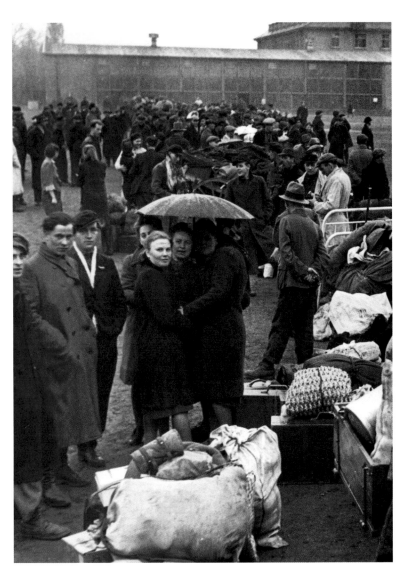

▶ *These displaced people in a refugee camp in 1945 are waiting to move to another camp. After World War II, there were 800,000 displaced persons living in camps in Germany and Austria.*

In the 1960s and 1970s, large movements of refugees took place in Africa and Asia. In many African countries, wars of independence were fought against the European rulers. One of the bloodiest conflicts was in Algeria (1954–1962). Many Algerians fled the violence for Morocco and Tunisia. In Asia, the war in Bangladesh in 1971 and the conflicts in Cambodia, Laos, and Vietnam created further waves of refugees.

The 1980s brought new wars, displacing people in northeast Africa, Asia, and Central America. The largest number of refugees came from Afghanistan. Following the Soviet invasion in 1979, more than six million Afghans left for Iran and Pakistan. Emergencies in the 1990s included the flight of the Kurds from northern Iraq in 1991 and the violent breakup of Yugoslavia after 1991. In Africa, the genocide in Rwanda in 1994 led to the exodus of two million Rwandans. The majority of refugees today are forced to flee because of armed conflict in their country.

▲ *This refugee from Rwanda has just arrived in Benaco camp in Tanzania, 1994.*

FACT:
While Iran takes in 1 refugee for every 26 Iranians and Tanzania 1 for every 73 Tanzanians, the figure for Britain is 1 for every 972. For the United States it is 1 for every 578. The European Union, a collection of some of the richest countries in the world, hosts less than 5 percent of the world's refugee population.
Forced Migration Review, 2002

3. Fleeing War and Natural Disasters

Civil war

Modern warfare has an enormous impact on civilian populations. Civilians may try to get out of the way of the fighting or they may be forced to move by soldiers. Civil wars in poor countries cause the largest numbers of refugees and IDPs. These countries already have weak economies and the effects of war can bring them close to collapse.

▼ *Soldiers from the Sudanese People's Liberation Army, the southern rebel army in Sudan, going to battle during the civil war, 1995.*

Sudan in northern Africa has the worst case of internal displacement in the world. Since Sudan gained independence in 1956, the richer, mainly Muslim, Arab people of the north have dominated the country. They have held government power, backed by the Sudanese army.

Just before independence, African people of poorer southern Sudan formed a rebel army to fight the North. This led to civil war, which has continued on and off ever since. About 4 million people have had to leave their homes and move to another part of the country.

Today the Sudanese government imprisons those people who oppose it. As a result more than 350,000 people have fled. Without a long-lasting peace settlement, Sudanese people will continue leaving their homes to escape war.

▲ *The civil war in Sudan led to famine because people could not grow their crops. This picture shows people collecting grain dropped by a plane.*

"If there is food in the south, and the soldiers stop attacking, then we will go back, but not before."
Atak Atong, western Sudan, who had to leave his village in the south when it was attacked by progovernment forces

Fleeing genocide

Occasionally many thousands of people have to leave their home area or escape over borders to another country because of the fear of genocide. Genocide is the planned mass killing of an entire ethnic or religious group, perhaps the most vicious human action imaginable.

In 1975, a party called the Khmer Rouge, led by a man called Pol Pot, came to power in Cambodia in southeastern Asia. The party wanted to turn the whole country into a communist peasant society. Everyone had to work on the land for at least ten hours a day with little food. Between 1 and 2 million people died between 1975 and 1978. They were either murdered by the Khmer Rouge or died of disease or hunger. In 1978 a new government took over. The country was on the brink of famine and more than 200,000 refugees moved to the border with Thailand.

◀ These skulls form part of a memorial to help people remember those who were killed by the Khmer Rouge in Cambodia.

In 1994 genocide occurred in Rwanda in central Africa. The conflict was rooted in colonial history. When the Belgians ruled Rwanda, they encouraged rivalry between the Tutsi, the more powerful minority, and the Hutu, who were peasant farmers. The country gained independence in 1962, but the tensions continued.

▲ Rwandan refugees fleeing their country in July 1994 after the genocide. It is estimated that about 2 million people left the country.

After the Hutu president was assassinated in April 1994, Hutu soldiers started killing Tutsis and Hutus who did not support the ruling party. Up to 1 million men, women, and children—mostly Tutsis—were killed. About 400,000 refugees fled to Tanzania and Burundi. Then Tutsi rebel forces gained control of the country. About 2 million Hutus, many of whom had been involved in the genocide, fled to the Democratic Republic of Congo in fear of revenge attacks. When countries turn in on themselves in such a way there is no alternative but to escape.

> "We looked up at the Rwandan hills. The entire African landscape was awash with people, all headed our way."
> *Maureen Connelly, aid worker in Tanzania, April 1994*

Country under attack

If your country is invaded or bombed, the chances are that you'll try to reach a safe area or attempt to leave the country altogether.

Sierra Leone in West Africa experienced a decade of violence in the 1990s. In 1991, forces from neighboring Liberia called the Revolutionary United Front (RUF) invaded the country. The fighting uprooted more than a million people over the following three years.

By 1994 the RUF had weakened, but violence against civilians continued. There was more fighting in 1997 and 1998. By the end of 1998, more than 1 million Sierra Leoneans remained uprooted. About 400,000 of them became refugees in nearby countries. In 1999 a peace agreement was signed, but there was still considerable fighting and abuses of human rights.

There have now been so many refugee crises that sometimes countries refuse to allow refugees in.

▼ *This Afghani girl fled Afghanistan after the U.S. attacks in 2001. She is living in a refugee camp in Peshawar, Pakistan.*

case study·case study·case study·case study·case study

"I'm Zacharia Wurie and I come from Sierra Leone. My school days were the best period of my life.… At break time we went bicycling, or played soccer, or we told each other stories while sitting in the sun.…

"I thought that I could become a lawyer. But when I was in the eighth grade, some rebels came over the border from Liberia and started a war. They said they wanted to liberate the people, but that was not true. They killed people.… They burned the rich people's houses and stole everything.… Sometimes the soldiers did these things, too. I saw the people who had been killed on the streets by the rebels. Because of the situation I had to escape to the Netherlands in 1991."

War has plagued Afghanistan in southern Asia since 1979, and many refugees have fled from their homes. Today 1.4 million Afghan refugees live in Iran and 1.2 million in Pakistan. Another 300,000 Afghan people are displaced in their own country.

▼ *With the cold winter approaching, Afghani refugees living in this camp in Peshawar, Pakistan, had only tents to protect them.*

In 2001 the United States led a bombing campaign against Afghanistan. The aim was to root out the group that had organized the terrorist attacks of September 11, 2001. Pakistan and Iran—and the other four surrounding countries—had so many Afghani refugees already that this time they quickly closed their borders to new arrivals.

Natural disasters

A vicious cycle of war and natural disasters can cause huge movements of people. In sub-Saharan Africa there is often not enough water for crops, animals, and people. The result is a drought. During wartime, such problems become worse. People may not be able to tend their crops properly. The crops are then more likely to fail, leading to famine.

People usually show great strength and are very resourceful, making the best of difficult circumstances. Yet war makes coping with drought or famine even more difficult. It is hard to travel to find food and water. Food prices rise. Often fighting armies seize what food there is, leaving civilian populations hungry.

During the late 1970s and early 1980s in northeast Africa, war and famine led to mass movements of people. In 1984, a famine developed in Ethiopia. The world's television screens filled with horrifying pictures of starving people holding their weak, hungry children. There was a mass exodus of about 300,000 people to Sudan; others went to Somalia and Djibouti. It is thought that at least 1 million Ethiopians died.

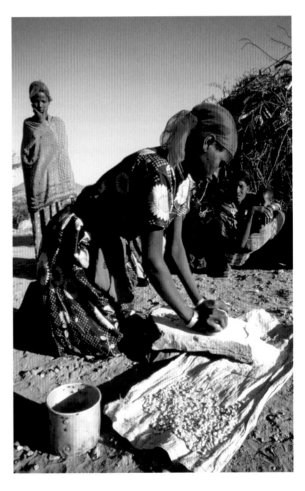

▼ *These Ethiopian refugees fled to Somalia in 1980 to avoid fighting in their country. The famine in 1984 led to a further exodus from Ethiopia.*

It was generally believed that drought and poor harvest caused the famine. Yet another central problem was war. Forces in Eritrea and Tigray, which were ruled by the Ethiopian government, were fighting for independence from Ethiopia. As part of the military campaign between 1980 and 1985, the Ethiopian army seized food supplies and rationed food for civilians. During the famine, Ethiopia would not allow international relief organizations to help people in areas controlled by the Eritrean and Tigrayan forces. This made the suffering even greater.

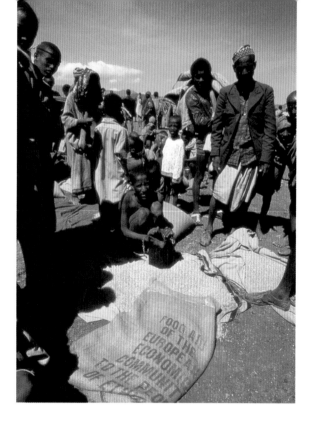

▲ Food aid from the European Community arriving in Ethiopia during the famine, 1984.

FACT:

Environmental projects can cause the mass displacement of people. In 2001 the Turkish government was planning to build the Ilisu Dam in southeast Turkey. The dam was to be built as part of a hydroelectric project to provide electrical power. It was going to affect 78,000 people, mostly Kurds. As many as 25,000 would have lost their homes, land, and livelihoods. Their land and villages would have been flooded by the huge reservoir created by the dam. In 2002 the project was halted because of a large international campaign that put pressure on the construction companies involved and persuaded them to stop work.

4. Abuses of Human Rights

Abuse and persecution

According to the 1951 UN definition, refugees are people fleeing persecution. These are people whose human rights are not respected in their own countries.

Examples of these refugees are people fighting for an independent state within their country, or those who oppose their governments when it is forbidden to do so.

Other refugees may be from an ethnic minority that suffers from racism. They may follow a religion that is not accepted in their country. They may be involved in defending human rights as a teacher, doctor, or lawyer.

▶ *A member of the Tingui-Boto people taking part in a peaceful protest outside the Justice Ministry in Brazil, 2002. Members of several indigenous groups in Brazil were concerned about a new law that they believed was harmful to their interests.*

24

◄ Mayan refugees from Guatemala in El Porvenir refugee camp in Mexico, 1990. They left their country to escape violence. During the 1980s, there was a civil war in Guatemala over land and human rights. At least 20,000 Maya were killed by the army.

When human rights are seriously abused, the numbers of people fleeing the country increase.

In Colombia in South America there is a struggle between the government and opposition forces. In 2001 both the army and opposition groups committed human rights abuses. Civilians were the principal victims.

"The paramilitaries were pressuring me to collaborate with them: "Work with us or leave the area or die." But to join up with them means working against our neighbors. That's why we had to leave."

Displaced peasant farmer in Barrancabermeja, Colombia, who left his home in 1995

More than 300 people "disappeared" (usually taken away by the army, never to return, and presumably killed). More than 4,000 civilians were killed, mostly by paramilitary groups backed by the army. Large numbers of people were displaced and more than 1,700 people were kidnapped. It is no wonder that people caught up in such conflicts try to escape.

25

Opposing the government

In certain countries, it is illegal to oppose the government or join a trade union. Even so, some brave people may still be active in organizing unions or demonstrations, or producing antigovernment newspapers. These courageous acts may at some point mean they are likely to be thrown into prison or tortured. They may even receive death threats. So they make the agonizing decision to leave.

Human rights violations are a large problem in Zimbabwe in east Africa. Since about 1985 President Robert Mugabe has tried to prevent opposition and to increase his own power.

▲ *Riot police in Zimbabwe controlling crowds of voters during the 2002 elections. President Mugabe managed to crush the opposition and remain in power.*

case study·case study·case study·case study·case study

"I'm Simba from Zimbabwe. Six weeks after the elections in 2000, my wife and I were attacked by the police for being MDC supporters. I was held in prison for weeks and was tortured so badly that I lost track of time. After being dumped in the bush, I eventually returned home. My family scraped together the money for a plane ticket to Britain.

"Two weeks after I arrived, I found out that my wife had died because of the injuries she received during the attack. I applied for asylum in Britain and was sent to Wandsworth prison for 6 months. I had to stay in my cell for 23 hours a day. In the end I was refused asylum."

In 1999 a new political party, the Movement for Democratic Change (MDC), was formed. It proved very successful. When the MDC gained nearly half of the seats in the 2000 election, Mugabe sent the army and police to punish its voters. The following year, he declared that anyone caught criticizing him was to be sent to prison. Since 2000 many Zimbabweans who oppose Mugabe have fled abroad.

Myanmar (Burma) is another country that does not allow political opposition. In 1990 the National League for Democracy (NLD), led by Aung San Suu Kyi, won 82 percent of the seats in the parliamentary election. But the military government ignored the vote and put dozens of elected NLD leaders in prison, including Aung San Suu Kyi. Anyone who is suspected of opposition risks imprisonment, torture, and execution. In December 1999, there were 127,800 refugees living outside Myanmar (Burma).

▶ *Aung San Suu Kyi talking to activists fighting for democracy in 1996. In 2000 she was placed under house arrest (she could not leave her home) and was not released for nearly two years. In 2003 she was put back in prison.*

Ethnic cleansing

Sometimes people are forced to leave their country because they belong to an ethnic group that the rulers will no longer tolerate. The former country of Yugoslavia was made up of six different nations: Serbia, Croatia, Slovenia, Montenegro, Bosnia and Herzegovinia, and Albania. Within each nation lived different ethnic groups. When the government collapsed in 1991, war broke out among these ethnic groups. The most powerful group, the Serbs, conquered large parts of the country. Some of the worst fighting was in Bosnia and about 700,000 Bosnians fled.

The Serb leader, Slobodan Milosevic, wanted to remove all non-Serbs from the areas he conquered. Throwing out people from a different ethnic group became known as "ethnic cleansing." Many were driven out of their homes, put in prison, tortured, and executed. In the town of Srebenica, Bosnian Serb forces killed 7,000 Bosnian Muslim men and boys.

A region called Kosovo was taken over by the Serbs. Further conflict erupted in 1998 between Serb forces and the majority group in Kosovo, who were ethnic Albanians, people of Albanian origin.

▼ *This Albanian child is one of many who fled from their homes in Pristina, Kosovo, in 1999 after Serb forces took control of the region. The refugees are resting in a village just over the border in Macedonia.*

About 850,000 ethnic Albanians fled for their lives, mostly to neighboring countries. Some went to other European countries, including Britain.

For instance, in March 1999, Serb forces invaded the village of Zhegra in Kosovo. Fourteen civilians were killed before ethnic Albanian Mitant Zimani, her husband, and her children managed to escape to the hills. They began a 30-hour trek to safety in neighboring Macedonia. Across the border, Rexhep Murseli and her nine children—also ethnic Albanians—took them in.

In 2001, Slobodan Milosevic was put on trial as a war criminal for the death and destruction he caused by ethnic cleansing.

"We had to help. We are ethnic Albanians and these people needed us. We cooked together and slept on the floor.... But it was no problem. There really wasn't anything else to do."

Rexhep Murseli, Macedonia, 2001

▼ *Slobodan Milosevic (seated) at his trial for war crimes in The Hague, the Netherlands, 2001. The Serb leader was accused of being responsible for the murder of hundreds of ethnic Albanians and for forcing out about 800,000 people.*

5. Leaving for a Better Life

The rich-poor divide

The gap between rich and poor countries has been getting wider since the mid-1970s. Now it seems that the process of globalization is making the gap even larger. Giant multinational companies want to be able to produce goods and run services wherever they like, usually at the lowest cost. They believe this will bring down the price of goods, create jobs, and allow wealth to trickle down through society. Yet small producers, such as peasant farmers, cannot survive in competition with big companies.

For example, the Mexican government used to help farmers buy seeds and fertilizers. In the 1980s they stopped this aid. Mexican farmers could not compete with the huge farms in the United States and Canada. Many of them gave up their farms to become migrant (moving) farmworkers living in the United States.

▶ *An Afghani shoe seller at work in Pakistan. Afghanistan is one of the poorest countries in the world, and this man left the country to find more profitable work.*

The growing rich-poor divide causes many people worldwide to migrate to make a living. They are called "economic migrants." They are not seen as being in fear of persecution and are not classed as refugees.

Some Somali refugees who have fled their war-torn country, Somalia, are now living in camps in Dadaab, Kenya, in East Africa. They are not allowed to work outside the camps, and it is hard to set up businesses inside them. Many refugees rely for survival on money sent to them by family members working in other countries.

It could be argued that there is not a great difference between people with a genuine fear of persecution (refugees) and those who are forced to migrate abroad to make money so their families do not starve (economic migrants).

▲ *Migrant workers harvesting green peppers in California. The majority of migrant farm workers in the United States are immigrants.*

FACT
An average factory worker in the United States earns about four times as much as a Mexican factory worker and 30 times as much as a Mexican agricultural worker.
New York Times, July 18, 2000

Economic crisis

Polish factory workers earn about $250 a month. On their summer vacations, some pick asparagus in Germany where they can earn about $830 a month. After communism collapsed in the Soviet Union and Eastern Europe in the early 1990s, many people found that their incomes dropped and they lost the benefits of a government welfare system. Thousands began to come to western Europe to find work.

However, in 1992 a single European community was created in Western Europe. It became the European Union in 1993. People from within the community were allowed to move freely between member countries to live and work. At the same time it became harder and harder for people from other lands, including Eastern Europe, to migrate legally to the European Union.

◀ *Kurdish refugees arriving in Italy by boat, 2002. Despite the dangers, some Kurdish refugees will pay vast sums of money to people who can smuggle them into Italy. They are desperate to escape persecution and poverty.*

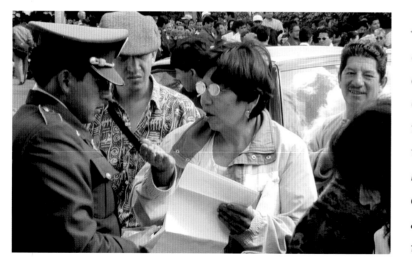

People in Ecuador lining up outside the Spanish embassy in the capital, Quito. They want to apply for a visa that will allow them to work in Spain. In Ecuador, about 70 percent of the people cannot afford the basic things they need to live.

In many developed countries, migrant workers cannot enter freely, yet it is accepted that they will come, often illegally, to take low-paying jobs such as farmwork that locals do not want to do.

Cubans fleeing Fidel Castro's communist regime for the United States after 1959 used to be welcomed with open arms. They were accepted as political refugees who preferred the American way of life to communism. In the early 1990s, the Soviet Union broke up and could no longer give support to its communist ally, Cuba. As poverty increased in Cuba, greater numbers of Cubans left for the United States. In 1994, with thousands of Cuban refugees arriving, the U.S. government decided they would no longer be accepted. Instead, new refugees would be placed in detention camps.

FACT

There are many illegal Eastern European migrants working in Britain. Wages for unskilled work are as low as $165–$265 a month. A worker earning the legal minimum wage would earn about $1097.41 a month for a 35-hour week (before paying taxes).

The debate about migration

The United States is a wealthy country, built by people from all around the world. The biggest groups are whites, African-Americans, Asians, Hispanics (people from Latin American countries living in the United States) and Native Americans. Historically, the United States has welcomed refugees and is a "melting pot" of different cultures. Europe is also a wealthy region. Its population has been falling as fewer children are born, so more workers are needed to keep the economies going. So why are refugees and immigrants rarely welcomed nowadays?

In the 1960s unemployment grew in Europe and the United States. Since then, immigrants have often been blamed for unemployment. The argument was that if there were no immigrants, there would be enough jobs for local people. Politicians then introduced immigration controls. This call to keep out foreigners has now extended to asylum seekers, who need refuge from persecution.

▶ *A boat from the Norwegian ship,* Tampa, *which rescued nearly 300 Afghani refugees from their sinking craft in the Indian Ocean in 2001. The refugees were trying to get to Australia, but Australia would not accept them.*

A demonstration in support of asylum seekers outside a detention center in Sydney, Australia, in 2002. Inside, asylum seekers had been on a hunger strike (refusing to eat). They were protesting the length of time it took for their applications for asylum to be processed.

In the United States, many European countries, and Australia, people who want to apply for asylum are locked up in detention centers as soon as they arrive. They are treated with suspicion and commonly seen as criminals trying to cheat their way into the country rather than people with a genuine fear of persecution. They have to prove that they really are escaping from a murderous regime before they are allowed to stay.

"An increase in workers usually expands the economy and so increases the jobs available for native workers.... That is why a million Cubans lifted the economy of Miami out of slump, and a million French colonists returning from Algeria [1962] lifted the south of France."

Nigel Harris, professor of Urban Economics, University College, London, 2000

In the media, refugees are often referred to as "swamping" the country with a huge "wave" of foreigners. People are led to believe that their numbers are far higher than they actually are. They may become concerned that their country cannot afford to support the newcomers, and this can lead to bad feelings toward refugees and even racism.

35

6.Without a Homeland

Longing for their land

Most refugees want to return home as quickly as possible. But sometimes they do not have a homeland to go to. Sometimes their country has been taken over by other people and they are no longer welcome there.

In 1948 the State of Israel was formed. It was a country for Jewish people, who did not previously have a homeland. That year the surrounding Arab countries started a war that Israel won. Israel took 78 percent of the land. Out of about 1.3 million Palestinian Arabs, nearly 1 million were driven from their homes and land. Most went to areas called the West Bank and Gaza Strip or to nearby Arab countries. The majority found shelter in refugee camps. During a later war in 1967, Israel conquered the West Bank and Gaza Strip, too. Following that war many Jewish refugees from around the world were welcomed in Israel.

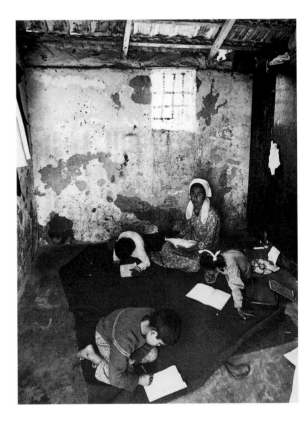

▶ *A Palestinian family living in Jabaliya refugee camp in the Gaza Strip. Because of curfews, the children cannot go to school and have to study at home.*

▲ *Palestinian women protesting in 2001 because Israeli soldiers have taken over a house in the West Bank to use as a base for their operations, forcing people from their homes.*

More than 50 years after Israel was founded, most refugees in the West Bank and Gaza Strip still live in tiny makeshift homes in refugee camps, with no running water. At the end of 2001, more than half of the Palestinians in the West Bank and Gaza Strip could not afford to buy the basic things they needed to live. The Palestinians have fought two uprisings against Israeli rule and have murdered Israeli citizens. The Israelis have responded by destroying their homes, stopping them from traveling freely, and killing people. The Palestinians hope that eventually they will win their own state.

"In 1948, our village near Nazareth was attacked by the Israeli army. I was six at the time. We fled to Ain al-Hilweh in Lebanon. My ten-year-old brother got lost in the rush and we've never seen him since. I don't suppose we'll ever be able to return. But I've still got the key to our old house."

Joumana, Palestinian refugee living in Lebanon

Fighting for freedom

Struggles between the government and groups that are fighting for their own independent state can lead to massive internal displacement and refugee movements. For instance, more than 20 million Kurdish people live in Iraq, Turkey, Iran, Syria, and Armenia. The Kurds are an ethnic minority in all these countries, with their own culture and way of life. They have no nation of their own but are struggling for an independent homeland. In Iraq the Kurds were persecuted by Saddam Hussein's armed forces.

After Iraq was defeated in the Gulf War of 1991, the Kurds rebelled. Iraqi forces then attacked them. About 1.3 million fled to Iran. Another 450,000 trekked through the mountains to the border with Turkey, but Turkey would not let them in. A "safe haven" for the Kurds was established in northern Iraq. However, Kurds worry that the Iraqi government might try once more to take control of the Kurdish regions.

◀ Kurdish refugees fleeing Iraq in 1991. They had joined the unsuccessful rebellion against the Iraqi dictator, Saddam Hussein. He then took revenge on the rebels. The 2003 war in Iraq brought an end to Saddam Hussein's rule, but the Kurds in Iraq still face an uncertain future.

In Turkey the Kurds are not recognized as a people. They are forbidden to speak their language or practice their culture. Kurdish books, poetry, and holidays are all illegal. During the 1990s, the Kurdistan Workers Party (PKK) led an uprising against Turkish rule. The Turkish army destroyed thousands of Kurdish villages, displacing the inhabitants, in an attempt to stop people from supporting the PKK. The PKK ceased to exist in 2002, but the persecution of Kurds continues today.

▲ *Turkish forces enter the Kurdish region of northern Iraq, preparing to attack Kurdish guerrilla fighters from the PKK, 1995. During the 1990s, the Turkish army often entered the region, which was outside Iraq's control, to fight the PKK.*

A few thousand Kurds managed to escape and seek asylum in Europe. Until they can live freely and safely in Turkey and Iraq, there will be further movements of refugees and displaced people.

FACT
About 3,000 Kurdish teachers, trade unionists, and other professionals have been killed by death squads in Turkey.
KurdishMedia.com 2002

7.Going Home

Choosing to go home

Most refugees have strong memories of their homeland throughout their years in exile. What they want above all is for the conflict there to end so that they can go home. When this happens, it is called voluntary repatriation. Repatriation means going back to your country.

Refugees often want to go back so much that they return even if the situation is still not entirely safe. They may have no homes or land to go back to, and there may be no basic facilities such as water or electricity supplies. Yet they return anyway. In June 1999, a peace plan for Kosovo (see pages 28–29) was agreed on. Within three weeks, 500,000 Kosovan Albanians had returned. By the end of 1999, more than 820,000 had gone back. It was the quickest return of refugees in history.

▼ *These Kosovan Albanian children returned to Kosovo in 1999 to find that their homes had been destroyed by Serb forces. The Albanians made huge efforts to rebuild their homes, hospitals, schools, and roads.*

After Ethiopia took over Eritrea in East Africa in 1962, there was a bitter 30-year civil war. From 1967 onward, about 500,000 people were forced to flee to neighboring Sudan, another poor country. About 25 percent settled in refugee camps. In 1993 Eritrea achieved independence but then there was another war between Ethiopia and Eritrea, which ended in 2000. Finally, in 2001 the refugees started to return from Sudan.

▶ *Eritrean refugees shaking hands with friends as the train leaves to take them back home, after 30 long years in refugee camps in Sudan.*

case study·case study·case study·case study·case study

"My name is Kidane Maasho. I fled Eritrea with my wife two decades ago after our village was bombed by Ethiopian warplanes. Thirteen of our neighbors were murdered by soldiers. We escaped through the desert, pushing our herd of 20 cattle, donkeys, and goats. In Sudan, we had to sell our herd to survive and then we had to move into a refugee camp. There was no work and nothing to do. But we made friends and raised seven children there.

"Now we have returned to Eritrea. I have been waiting for this day for 20 years. Sudan has been very good to me and my family. I thank my God for keeping me long enough to see this day. I am old and weak, but I have finally made it home."

Forced to go home

Sometimes refugees are forced to return home against their will. Most refugees are "pushed" to go home. The host states—the countries where they are living—stop helping them. Or they are "pulled" by promises of land or improved human rights if they go home, promises that may not be fulfilled. If they have lived in exile for many years, they may have settled, raised families, and become part of a new community. Forcing them to go back means uprooting them once more.

Some refugees may have nowhere to go back to. Their homes and communities may have been destroyed. If there has been "ethnic cleansing," they may no longer be welcome in the area.

◀ *Rohingya refugees lining up for water in Dumdumia camp on the Bangladesh-Myanmar (Burma) border in 1992. The Rohingya were forced to go back to Myanmar (Burma) even though it was not safe for them to do so.*

In 1991–1992, 250,000 Muslim refugees, known as the Rohingya, fled from Buddhist Myanmar (Burma) to Muslim Bangladesh to escape serious human rights abuses (see page 27). They lived in refugee camps there. But Bangladesh is very poor. At first, the refugees were helped. But in late 1992, tens of thousands were forced to go back. They were told their food rations would be cut and were threatened with violence if they did not return. The Rohingya returned to continuing human rights abuses in Myanmar (Burma) and some had to flee once more.

After the genocide in Rwanda in 1994, about 580,000 people fled to neighboring Tanzania. In December 1996, the Tanzanian government and the UN High Commissioner for Refugees stated that all refugees could return to Rwanda in safety. Refugee leaders did not agree. The Tanzanian government used troops to force the refugees across the border into Rwanda.

> "It was like trying to load the ark two by two, but the waters had already reached shoulder level."
>
> *Aid official trying to control the flow of Rwandan refugees returning from Zaire in 1996*

▼ *These Rwandan refugees were forced by Tanzanian soldiers at gunpoint to return to Rwanda in late 1996. Here they are crossing Rusomo Bridge on the Rwandan border.*

The future

While there are conflicts, human rights abuses, and natural disasters, there will always be people forced to flee and become refugees. During the 20th century, warfare came to mean all-out war against civilian populations, enormously increasing the numbers displaced by conflict. Global warming means that floods and other environmental problems are likely to become worse. They will cause further movements of population.

For those refugees who manage to escape to another country, the difficulties are mounting. The poor countries that receive the majority of refugees suffer from a lack of resources. In richer countries, new harsh rules make it harder for refugees to enter and gain permission to stay.

Refugees can make an important contribution to the countries where they live. Some refugees have become world famous, such as Albert Einstein, a Jewish scientist who fled the Nazis in 1933. Duc Tran was a refugee from Vietnam who built a huge business empire importing popular Asian fruits to the United States.

▲ *A demonstration against the poor treatment of asylum seekers in London, 2001. The slogan "hands off my friend" was the name of the campaign. It was supported by trade unions, student groups, celebrities, and many other people.*

Refugees bring a wealth of skills, talents, and culture and play a valuable role in their new country. Maybe you are a refugee yourself or have refugees at your school. Many of the people you know will have parents, grandparents, or great-grandparents who were refugees.

Is there a solution to the issue of refugees? Closing the huge rich-poor divide between and within countries would certainly help to reduce conflict in the world and the need to escape from it. In the meantime, many organizations are helping refugees, campaigning to improve their rights, and informing the public about why they have fled. As individuals, we can join them to extend a warm welcome to those escaping persecution and terror in their own land.

> "Elis is a great player and he's really friendly. He's just like anyone. He's just like us."
>
> *Kevin McArron, 14, about his soccer teammate Elis Suferi, a 13-year-old asylum seeker from Macedonia.*

▼ *The victorious Somali team in the National Football [soccer] Festival, a competition for London's refugee communities.*

GLOSSARY

assassination
killing of a famous or important person for political reasons

asylum seekers
refugees who claim the right to live in safety in another country because they have been persecuted in their own land

civil war
war between groups of people in the same country

civilian
person who is not in the armed forces or the police force

colonialism
practice of one country ruling over another country or area

communism
system of government in which the government, not individual people, controls the production of goods and the running of services

convention
official agreement between countries or leaders

detention camp or **center**
place where refugees are held while it is decided whether they are allowed to stay in the country

drought
long period of time when little or no rain falls

economic migrant
person who moves to another country to make a better living

emigrate
to leave one's country of birth to live in a new country

ethnic group
group of people who share a common culture, tradition, and sometimes language

ethnic minority
group of people who have a different culture, religion, language, or skin color from most other people in their society

exodus
many people leaving a place at the same time

famine
lack of food in a region over a long period of time

genocide
deliberate killing of everyone of a particular ethnic group

global warming
increase in temperature of the earth's atmosphere

globalization
breaking down of all barriers to the movement of money or goods between countries, in theory turning the whole world into a single economic unit

guerrilla group
band of nonprofessional fighters that make war against a regular army

homeland
country where a person was born. Some people, such as the Kurds and the Palestinians, do not control their own homeland.

human rights
rights to basic human needs such as a home, food, work, health care, and education. Also included are political rights, such as the right to vote. The UN Convention on Human Rights states that countries have to respect these rights.

immigration
coming to live in a new country

immigration controls
rules that limit the number of immigrants that can come into a country from certain other countries

internally displaced person (IDP)
person who has been forced to leave the area where he or she lived and move to a different part of the same country

migrant
someone who moves from one country or region to another

military government
government controlled by the armed forces

nation-state
independent country formed by people who share the same culture and language

paramilitaries
military groups that help the official army of a country.

persecuted
harrassed or repeatedly treated badly

racism
prejudice or discrimination based on race. The belief that some races or superior to others.

ration
limited amount of something that people are allowed to have

refugee
person who has been forced to leave his or her country, usually because of war or persecution

relief organizations
groups, such as the Red Cross and Oxfam, that help out in an emergency

torture
inflicting of severe pain or suffering, whether physical or mental, on a person. Torture is used sometimes to obtain a confession, to intimidate, or to punish.

United Nations (UN)
association of many countries that aims to improve social conditions and to solve political problems in a peaceful way by consultation and negotiation

welfare
help such as money or services, given to needy people

FURTHER INFORMATION

ORGANIZATIONS

North America
American Red Cross
International Response Relief Fund
PO Box 37243
Washington, DC 20013
(202) 728-6477 or
800 HELP-NOW
www.redcross.org

Amnesty International USA
322 Eighth Avenue
New York, NY 10001
(212) 807-8400
www.aiusa.org

Canadian Council for Refugees
6839 Drolet #302
Montréal
Québec H2S 2T1
Canada
(514) 277-7223

National Network for Immigrant
and Refugee Rights
310 8th Street
Suite 303
Oakland, CA 94607
(510) 465-1984
www.nnirr.org

US Committee for Refugees
1717 Massachusetts Avenue, N.W.
Suite 200
Washington, DC 20036
(202) 347-3507
www.refugees.org

International
United Nations High Commissioner
for Refugees (UNHCR)
C.P. 2500
1211 Geneva
Switzerland
41 22 917 7817
www.unhcr.ch

BOOKS TO READ

Brooks, Philip. *Immigration.* Chicago: Heinemann, 2004.
Madocks, Steven. *Refugees.* Chicago: Raintree, 2004.
Trier, Jean. *United Nations High Commissioner for Refugees.* Parsippany, N.J.: Silver Burdett, 1995.

If you're interested in learning about refugees from a specific country, you might want to check out books in one of these two series:

In Their Own Voices (Rosen Publishing Group, New York)
Journey Between Two Worlds (Lerner Publihing Group, Minneappolis, MN)

INDEX